BIBLE REAING MARATHON No.3

Standing on

THE PROMISES OF GOD

A 26-Week Bible Reading Schedule

H is divine power has given us everything we need for life and godliness through our knowledge of him who called us by his own glory and goodness. 4 Through these he has given us his very great and precious promises, so that through them you may participate in the divine nature and escape the corruption in the world caused by evil desires.

-2 Peter 1:3-4 NKJV

Developed and Sponsored by the
Central Avenue Church of Christ
301 East Central Avenue - Valdosta, Georgia

Published by
Growing Panes

3543 Raintree Drive - Valdosta, GA 31601

Standing on
THE PROMISES OF GOD
A 26-WEEK BIBLE READING SCHEDULE

Published by
GROWING PANES, INC.
3543 Raintree Drive   *   Valdosta, Ga 31601

Copyright © 2014 Gresham R. Holton, Editor
grholton@yahoo.com

ISBN: 13 - 978-0-9905499-1-8
ISBN- 10:- 0990549917

ALL RIGHTS RESERVED
No part of this publication may be reproduced, stored in a retrieval system, or transmitted in any form by any means –electronic, mechanical, photocopying, recording or otherwise- without prior written consent.

Printed by CreateSpace, An Amazon.com Company
Available from Amazon.com, CreateSpace.com, and other retail outlets
2014

Bible Reading Marathon—No. 3

Standing on the Promises of God

(Reading Topics)	(Reading Dates)	(Page)
Taking Our Stand	☐ -Week 1:	8
The Promises of God	☐ -Week 2:	9
Only One God	☐ -Week 3:	10
Becoming Children of God	☐ -Week 4:	11
God is in us	☐ -Week 5:	12
Transformed in Christ	☐ -Week 6:	14
God Gives us Power	☐ -Week 7:	15
Freedom in Christ	☐ -Week 8:	16
Jesus: the Only Way	☐ -Week 9:	17
Strength when we are Weak	☐ -Week 10:	18
If we Seek We Will Find	☐ -Week 11:	19
Will Bear Fruit	☐ -Week 12:	20
God's Love	☐ -Week 13:	22
Our Love in Practice	☐ -Week 14:	24
Grace for Good Works	☐ -Week 15:	25
God will Give us Rest	☐ -Week 16:	26
Not Overcome by Temptations	☐ -Week 17:	27
Unity in Christ	☐ -Week 18:	28
Blessed for Reading God's Word	☐ -Week 19:	29
Train up a Child	☐ -Week 20:	30
Our Prayers will be Answered	☐ -Week 21:	31
Saved from Sin	☐ -Week 22:	32
One Hope in Christ	☐ -Week 23:	33
God will not Forsake us	☐ -Week 24:	34
A Guaranteed Inheritance	☐ =Week 25:	36
Life Eternal	☐ -Week 26:	37

Special Thanks

To the following dedicated students of the Bible who researched and compiled the Scripture passages for the 3rd Bible Reading Marathon. They are faithful members of the Central Avenue church of Christ in Valdosta, Georgia. Their work was reviewed and checked by two other people prior to publication.

Homer Anderson	Glenn Copeland	Kenny Holton	Marilyn King	Carrie Seat
Myra Anderson	Jerry Deloach	G. R. Holton	John Klimko	Don Seat
Kevin Boyd	O'Neal Grant	John Hunt	Bill Malone	Toni Webb
Byron Brown	Rachel Hayes	Bryan Jarvis	Debbie Paine	Marie Weeks
Janet Brown	Ruth Harrison	Larry Jonas	Mike Paine	Leon Weeks

Encouraging the Habit of Regular Bible Reading

It's a Matter of "HABIT"

A "habit" may be defined as "an acquired behavior pattern regularly followed until it has become almost involuntary: the habit of looking both ways before crossing the street; or the habit of brushing your teeth every morning". Habit formation is the process by which a behavior, through regular repetition, becomes automatic or habitual. Strong habits become almost compulsory.

As the habit is forming, it can be analyzed in three parts: the **cue**, the **behavior,** and the **reward**. The cue is the thing that causes your habit to come about, the trigger to your habitual behavior. This could be anything that your mind associates with that habit and you will automatically let a habit come to the surface. The behavior is the actual habit that you are exhibiting and the reward, a positive feeling, therefore continues the "habit loop." (from Charles Duhigg, *The Power of Habit).* A habit may initially be triggered by a goal, but over time that goal becomes less necessary and the habit becomes more automatic.

The ***Bible Reading Marathon*** is based on this three-part *"habit formation"* formula*:*

A. *The Cue,* or trigger that begins the habit-forming cycle. The Marathon schedule includes posted scriptures, a time-table for reading, and beginning and end cues.

B. *The Routine,* or the behavior patterns that must become repetitive over time. On a regular (or daily) basis you will repeat the same behavior, i. e. complete the Bible reading schedule.

C. *The Rewards,* or the positive, good feeling you experience for completing the behavior and completing the course. In addition, runners in the Bible Reading Marathon enjoy the knowledge of being blessed by pleasing God.

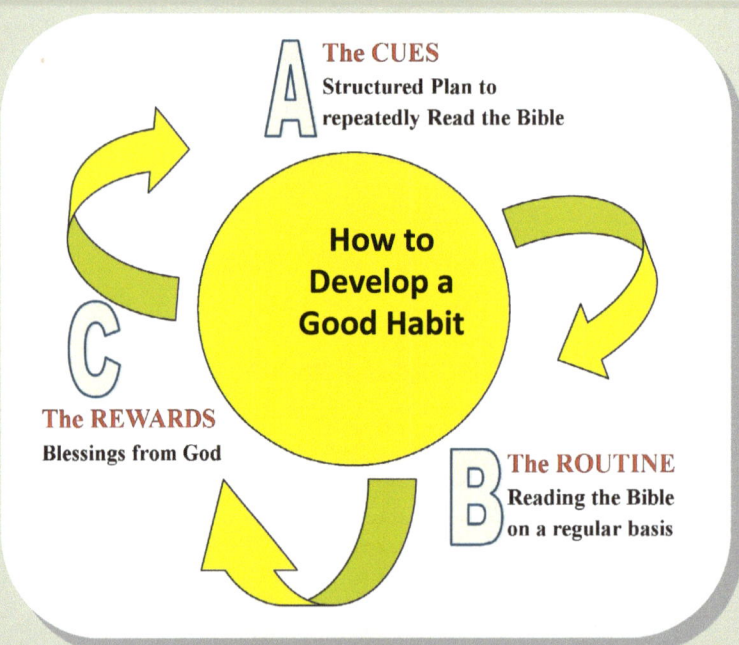

The Bible Reading Marathon is just *a tool* to help you develop the habit of regularly reading your Bible! Strong "good" habits are just as hard to break as bad habits. Regular Bible reading is a good habit. Use the next twenty-six weeks to form the habit of regular Bible reading!

THE PROMISES OF GOD

"*Standing on the Promises of God*" is the topic of the 3rd Bible Reading Marathon. Marathon runners will read and study twenty-six of the 3513 promises of God written in the Bible (www.bibleinfo.com). Our purpose is to develop and maintain the habit of regularly reading the Bible, God's inspired Word.

These are *God's promises!* You can count on Him. "*You know with all your heart and soul that not one of all the good promises the Lord your God gave you has failed. Every promise has been fulfilled; not one has failed*"(Joshua 23:14, NIV). Your faith in God is both the motivation and the result of reading and living His Word. That belief and trust in His divine power is what caused you to enter the Bible Reading Marathon.

God desires *good* for you not evil! Reading His Word will explain to you numerous opportunities to *do good*. This is a win-win situation, with no harm! *"For Jehovah God is our Light and our Protector. He gives us grace and glory. No good thing will He withhold from those who walk along his paths."*(Psalm 84:11, TLB).

God will *help you!* Go to the Scriptures with a submissive prayerful attitude to know God, and His Will *will be* revealed! *"If any of you lacks wisdom, let him ask of God, who gives to all liberally and without reproach, and it will be given to him"*(James 1:5, NKJV).

Reading the Bible regularly is like a cool breeze on a hot day. We are all challenged by the daily cares of living in a fallen world. Anxiety often dominates our minds and stresses our lives. God's Word is good like a "balm in Gilead", it restores the soul. *"You keep him in perfect peace whose mind is stayed on you, because he trusts in you"* (Isaiah 26:3 ESV).

Do you feel that you have lost control? Are you discouraged by your inability to withstand the pressures? The bombardment of evil and sin in our lives may cause us to just want to "give up"… to "throw in the towel"! Your faith in God's promises will help you stand*!* *"No temptation has overtaken you but such as is common to man; and God is faithful, who will not allow you to be tempted beyond what you are able, but with the temptation will provide the way of escape also, so that you will be able to endure it* (1 Corinthians 10:13 NASB).

All this will be over some day along with the pain and suffering of the flesh. Now is the time to build a relationship with your Maker. God has promised to *"wipe away every tear from their eyes, and death shall be no more, neither shall there be mourning nor crying nor pain any more, for the former things have passed away (Revelation 21:4 RSV)."*

Reading your Bible is like reading about your dream home. Compared with your current "tent" it is going to be a "mansion" with many rooms! *"In my Father's house are many mansions; if it were not so, I would have told you; for I go to prepare a place for you. And if I go and prepare a place for you, I will come again, and will receive you unto myself; that where I am, there ye may be also (John 14:2-3 ASV)"*

This is just a sampling of the promises of God…from different translations of the Bible!

-GRH

Reading the Bible is Your Choice!

God expects His people to read His Word. *"But regarding the resurrection of the dead, have you not read what was spoken to you by God: 'I AM THE GOD OF ABRAHAM, AND THE GOD OF ISAAC, AND THE GOD OF JACOB'? He is not the God of the dead but of the living* (Matthew 22:31-32 NKJV).

Readers will be blessed. *"All Scripture is given by inspiration of God, and is profitable for doctrine, for reproof, for correction, for instruction in righteousness, that the man of God may be complete, thoroughly equipped for every good work"* (2 Timothy 3:16-17 NKJV). In addition, reading the Bible will prepare Christians to do good work.

Like any good exercise program, reading your Bible will take a commitment of time and effort on your part. How much time will you devote to your readings? How involved will you become in really studying God's Word? Are you willing to pray that God will give you the wisdom to understand it? These are issues you must resolve to be a successful Marathon runner.

The Bible Reading Marathon program is designed to simplify your choices. The Greek Marathon is the base model for this plan. It was a run of 42.195 kilometers, or 26 miles. Unlike other races, the Marathon demands personal commitment and an ability to endure. More than 500 "Marathons" are run each year. Anyone can run in a "Marathon", regardless of your age or gender. The "winners" are all those who finish the race, rather than just a single person.

The Greek Marathon was probably in the mind of God when he had the writer of Hebrews pen these words: *" Therefore, since we are surrounded by such a great cloud of witnesses, let us throw off everything that hinders and the sin that so easily entangles. And let us run with perseverance the race marked out for us,"* (Hebrews 12:1 NIV).

Chose which Track you will Run

Inside Track:

- If you do not think you have the time or discipline to read more, start by regularly reading a few verses on the **Inside Track**.
- This track is also for the children who are just now entering "the Race".
- Read only the Scriptures in the first column of the schedule

Reading Time: 1-3 minutes

1-7 Verses Daily
approx. 910 verses in 26 weeks

Middle Lanes:

- If you are a new Christian, or if you have not developed the habit of regular Bible reading, the **Middle Lanes** may be for you.
- The majority of "runners" will probably choose this track.
- Read *all the scriptures in both the Inside Track and the Middle Lanes.*

Reading Time: 3 - 10 minutes

20-30 verses Daily
approx. 3900 verses in 26 weeks

Fast Track:

- The **Fast Track** is for the serious Reading Marathon runners who already have a strong habit of regular Bible Reading.
- You are willing to dedicate the time and effort for 26 weeks!
- Read *all scriptures in all three lanes: Inside Track, Middle Lanes and Fast Track.*

Reading Time: 20-30 minutes

30-50 verses Daily
approx. 6500 verses in 26 weeks

"Exercise" with a Friend...or Several Friends!

As iron sharpens iron,
So a man sharpens the countenance of his friend. (Proverbs 27:17)

Any exercise program, especially a spiritual exercise program, is best with a friend. Friends support each other. A friend will be truthful and direct with us. Just to have another trusted individual with you when you discover some new exciting truth makes it more exciting! We all have a friend who *"sticks closer than a brother"* (Proverbs 18:24). Recruit that friend to join you in running the Bible Reading Marathon. Or...run the Marathon with an entire congregation of Christians!

A Running "Partner"

Your life partner, your mate, may be the person you want to recruit. This is especially true if he or she is not a Christian! If you are like most people, talking to your mate about *"religious things"* is difficult especially if your mate does not share your faith. A godly wife has a tremendous influence: *"Wives, likewise, be submissive to your own husbands, that even if some do not obey the word, they, without a word, may be won by the conduct of their wives, when they observe your chaste conduct accompanied by fear."* (1 Peter 3:1-2). But, a husband and wife do enjoy doing things together!

Your neighbor next door, or your friend who meets you at the gym on a regular basis to exercise, or even a loving relative!

It might be somewhat less personal, but just as effective to recruit your "friends" on the social networks. Post a notice of what you plan to do the next twenty-six weeks, and ask your "friends" to join you. Then, as you read about the Promises of God you can post your impressions, or what you have learned, or other information that will generate discussion. (Be sure your friends have a copy of the Bible Reading Marathon reading schedule.)

Your "Church" Friends...

Imagine the results if all the members of the church where you worship were reading about the ***Promises of God*** together! It would promote unity and encourage fellowship! The "Promises" could become the topic for Bible classes, or the schedule for pulpit sermons. More than that, when we take our stand on the Word of God we are on solid religious grounds! Many Christians need to re-study where they stand concerning their faith! The twenty-six week marathon could actually fire a 21st Century revival in the congregation!

Involving the entire church is a as simple as "A, B, C":

A. Set a ***beginning date and an ending date.***

B. Ask everyone to ***Make the Commitment*** to participate in the Marathon. Even the children and those "very busy" can take the *Inside Track* to read just a few verses each day.

C. ***Promote the importance*** of the Marathon by reporting on the weekly progress. That may be as simple as posting the <u>actual number</u> that read, or it could be the <u>percentage</u> of those who committed to read. We all like to know "how we are doing" in any race.

For bodily exercise profits a little, but godliness is profitable for all things, having promise of the life that now is and of that which is to come.
(1 Timothy 4:8)

3rd Bible Reading Marathon

WEEK 1: [Dates:..........................] **PROMISES OF GOD:** *Taking Our Stand on the Promises of God*

INSIDE TRACK	MIDDLE LANES	FAST TRACK	
Monday: ☐ Joshua 1:1-5 ☐	**Monday:** ☐ Amos 3:1-15 ☐ Matthew 7:13-23 ☐	**Monday:** ☐ John 14:15-24 ☐ Romans 6:1-23 ☐ Hebrews 11:1-12; 32-40 ☐ Matthew 25:31-46 ☐ 1 John 2:3 ☐ 2 Chronicles 7:14 ☐	**TRUST AND OBEY** _____ _____ _____ _____ _____ _____ _____
Tuesday: ☐ Joshua 1:6-7 ☐	**Tuesday:** ☐ Esther 4:1-17 ☐ Acts 4:7-20 ☐	**Tuesday:** ☐ 1 John 1:4-7 ☐ Deut 31:6 ☐ 2 Timothy 1:7-8 ☐ 1 Corinthians 16:13 ☐ Acts 20:22-24 ☐ Nehemiah 6:10-13 ☐ Ephesians 6:10-18	**COURAGE TO STAND** _____ _____ _____ _____ _____ _____
Wednesday: ☐ Joshua 1:8 ☐	**Wednesday:** ☐ Psalms 1 ☐ Deut. 6:1-9 ☐	**Wednesday:** ☐ Proverbs 3:5-6 ☐ Proverbs 16:12 ☐ 1 Timothy 4:13-14 ☐ Psalms 119:2,15,18 ☐ 2 Timothy 2:2 ☐ ☐	**MEDITATE ON GOD'S WORD** _____ _____ _____ _____ _____ _____
Thursday: ☐ Joshua 1:9-11 ☐	**Thursday:** ☐ 1 Chronicles 28:10-20 ☐ 1 Kings 2:1-4 ☐	**Thursday:** ☐ Matthew 7:21 ☐ Romans 8:31-39 ☐ Jude 1:1-25 ☐ 1 Peter 5:8-10 ☐ James 4:7-10 ☐ ☐	**STAND WITH GOD** _____ _____ _____ _____ _____
Friday: ☐ Joshua 24:15 ☐ Judges 21:25	**Friday:** ☐ Isaiah 1:1-31 ☐ Matthew 4:1-25 ☐	**Friday:** ☐ Judges 4:18-22 ☐ Zeckariah 3:1-2 ☐ Revelation 12:9 ☐ 2 Corinthians 4:4 ☐ 1 John 4:4 ☐ John 13:21-30 ☐ Revelation 12:11-12	**SUCCESS OR FAILURE** _____ _____ _____

"Within the covers of the Bible are the answers for all the problems men face."

— Ronald Reagan

3rd Bible Reading Marathon

WEEK 2: [Dates:..........................] PROMISES OF GOD: *God Has Promised*

INSIDE TRACK	MIDDLE LANES	FAST TRACK	
Monday:	**Monday:**	**Monday:**	*GREAT PROMISES*
☐ 2 Peter 1:3-4	☐ John 3:14-18	☐ Genesis 12:1-3	
☐	☐ Matthew 11:25-30	☐ Deuteronomy 28:1-14	
	☐ John 10:27-30	☐ 2 Samuel 7:8-17	
		☐ Hebrews 6:10-19	
		☐ Hebrews 9:8-15	
		☐ Hebrews 12:18-29	
Tuesday:	**Tuesday:**	**Tuesday:**	*GUARANTEED PROMISES*
☐ Eph 1:13-14	☐ Acts 2:32-40	☐ Hebrews 10:10-25	
☐	☐ 2 Peter 1:5-11	☐ Psalm 19:7-14	
	☐ 2 Peter 3:3-13	☐ Hebrews 13:5-8	
		☐ Romans 8:31-39	
Wednesday:	**Wednesday:**	**Wednesday:**	*PARTAKERS OF THE DIVINE NATURE*
☐ 2 Cor 1:20-22	☐ Genesis 1:25-31	☐ Ephesians 1:16 – 2:7	
☐	☐ Ephesians 4:22 – 5:1	☐ Hebrews 2:6-16	
	☐ Psalm 8:1-9	☐ 1 John 2:28 – 3:3	
Thursday:	**Thursday:**	**Thursday:**	*ESCAPE THE CORRUPTIONS OF THE WORLD*
☐ 2 Cor 7:1	☐ 1 John 3:4-16	☐ Hebrews 6:1-9	
☐	☐ 2 Corinthians 6:14-18	☐ 1 Peter 1:13-25	
		☐ 1 Peter 2:1-17	
Friday:	**Friday:**	**Friday:**	*ALL THINGS ARE POSSIBLE!*
☐ Matt 19:24-27	☐ Genesis 18:9-15	☐ Romans 4:13-25	
☐	☐ John 11:38-44	☐ John 5:19-29	
		☐ Romans 8:18-30	

"A thorough knowledge of the Bible is worth more than a college education."

-Theodore Roosevelt

3rd Bible Reading Marathon

WEEK 3: [Dates:...........................] **PROMISES OF GOD:** *Only One God*

INSIDE TRACK	MIDDLE LANES	FAST TRACK	
Monday:	**Monday:**	**Monday:**	***CREATOR OF ALL THINGS***
☐ Genesis 1:1	☐ Romans 1:21-25	☐ Psalms 95:1-11	
☐	☐ I Peter 4:12-19	☐ Psalms 121: 1-8	
	☐ Isaiah 44:24-28	☐ Isaiah 42:4-6	
	☐ Ecclesiastes 11:4-6	☐ Deuteronomy 32:5-7	
		☐ Proverbs 22:1-3	
		☐ Jeremiah. 51:18-20	
		☐ Jeremiah. 10:15-16	
Tuesday:	**Tuesday:**	**Tuesday:**	***FATHER OF US ALL***
☐ Ephesians 4:6	☐ Matthew 25:33-35	☐ Acts 3:13-26	
☐	☐ Romans 1:1-7	☐ Romans 6:3-5	
	☐ I John 2:12-14	☐ Romans 8:14-16	
	☐ I John 3:1-3	☐ I Corinthians 8:5-7	
		☐ Galatians 1:3-5	
		☐ Ephesians 3:13-21	
		☐ I Peter 1:1-3	
Wednesday:	**Wednesday:**	**Wednesday:**	***ONE LAWGIVER***
☐ James 4:12	☐ Exodus 13:8-10	☐ Romans 2:12-16	
☐ Isaiah 33:21-23	☐ Leviticus 18:25-27	☐ Galatians 5:13-26	
	☐ Joshua 24:14-18	☐ Galatians 6:1-3	
	☐ Romans 10:3-5	☐ I Timothy 1:8-11	
		☐ Hebrews 10:15-17	
		☐ James 2:7-9	
		☐ I John 3:4-6	
Thursday:	**Thursday:**	**Thursday:**	***NO OTHER GOD EXCEPT HIM***
☐ Jere. 2:11-13	☐ Exodus 20:2-5	☐ II Kings 17:34-38	
☐	☐ Deuteronomy 5:6-10	☐ II Chronicles 32:16-23	
	☐ Judges 10:11-16	☐ Jeremiah 7:1-8	
		☐ Jeremiah 44:1-6	
		☐ Psalms 16:1-11	
		☐	
		☐	
Friday:	**Friday:**	**Friday:**	***WORSHIP HIM ONLY***
☐ 1 Cor.10:20-21	☐ Psalms 100:1-5	☐ Revelation 14:6-14	
☐	☐ Daniel 3:28-29	☐ Luke 4:5-13	
	☐ Matthew 4:8-10	☐ Hebrews 1:5-14	
		☐ Revelation 4:9-11	

The Bible is one of the greatest blessings bestowed by God on the children of men. It has God for its author; salvation for its end, and truth without any mixture for its matter. It is all pure.

-John Locke

3rd Bible Reading Marathon

WEEK 4: [Dates:...........................] **PROMISES OF GOD:** *Be Children of God*

INSIDE TRACK

Monday:
- [ ] 1 John 3:1
- [ ]

Tuesday:
- [ ] Gal 3:26-27
- [ ]

Wednesday:
- [ ] 1 John 3:18-19
- [ ] Psalms 26:3

Thursday:
- [ ] Hebrews 6:1-3
- [ ]

Friday:
- [ ] Rom 8:16-17
- [ ] Hosea 1:9-11

MIDDLE LANES

Monday:
- [ ] Luke 20:35-37
- [ ] Romans 8:13-22
- [ ] Matthew 5:8-10

Tuesday:
- [ ] Galatians 3:7-27
- [ ] I John 2:28-29
- [ ] I John 3:8-10

Wednesday:
- [ ] John 15:9-11
- [ ] Ecclesiastes 12:13-14
- [ ] Luke 8:9-15
- [ ] Hebrews 5:7-14
- [ ] Joshua 24:13-15

Thursday
- [ ] Hosea 1:9-11
- [ ] Luke 20:34-38
- [ ] John 1:11-13
- [ ] Titus 3:1-11

Friday
- [ ] Luke 20:34-38
- [ ] John 1:11-13
- [ ] Titus 3:1-11

FAST TRACK

Monday:
- [ ] I John 3:1-10
- [ ] I John 5:13-21
- [ ] Galatians 4:5-7
- [ ] John 8:40-42
- [ ] Romans 9:7-9
- [ ] Phillipians 2:14-16
- [ ] Hebrews 12:3-5

Tuesday:
- [ ] John 3:1-9
- [ ] I John 5:1-19
- [ ] Romans 3:24-31
- [ ] I Peter 1:23
- [ ] I John 4:7-9
- [ ] Romans 10:17
- [ ] Ephesians 2:8-10

Wednesday:
- [ ] I Peter 1:13-15
- [ ] John 14:15-31
- [ ] Psalms 101:5-7
- [ ] Hebrews 8:8-10
- [ ] I Peter 4:9-11
- [ ] Revelation 2:9-11
- [ ] Psalms 116:15

Thursday:
- [ ] Ephesians 4:11-32
- [ ] Phillipians 3:15-21
- [ ] Colossians 1:24-29
- [ ] James 1:2-8
- [ ]
- [ ]
- [ ]

Friday:
- [ ] Galatians 3:5-27
- [ ] Ephesians 3:1-12
- [ ] I Peter 3:7-12
- [ ]
- [ ]
- [ ]
- [ ]

SONS OF GOD

BORN AGAIN BY FAITH

OBEDIENT CHILDREN

GROWING CHILDREN

HEIRS OF GOD

*It ain't those parts of the Bible that I can't understand that bother me,
it is the parts that I do understand.*
-Mark Twain

3rd Bible Reading Marathon

WEEK 5: [Dates:..........................] PROMISES OF GOD: *God is in us*

INSIDE TRACK	MIDDLE LANES	FAST TRACK	
Monday: ☐ Galatians 2:20 ☐	**Monday:** ☐ 1 John 1:5-10 ☐ 1 John 3:1-24 ☐	**Monday:** ☐ John 17:20-26 ☐ 1 Corinthians 1:2-9 ☐ 2 Corinthians 13:5-11 ☐ Philippians 1:18-26 ☐ Colossians 3:1-4 ☐	**CHRIST ABIDES IN US**
Tuesday: ☐ John 15:4 ☐	**Tuesday:** ☐ John 14:6-11 ☐ Romans 6:1-23 ☐	**Tuesday:** ☐ 1 Corinthians 1:26-31 ☐ 1 Corinthians 6:17 ☐ 1 Corinthians 12:27-31 ☐ Ephesians 5:22-23 ☐ Colossians 2:6-12 ☐ 1 John 2:20-25 ☐	**WE ABIDE IN CHRIST**
Wednesday: ☐ John 15:5 ☐	**Wednesday:** ☐ John 15:1-17 ☐ Colossians 1:3-13 ☐	**Wednesday:** ☐ Psalms 1:1-6 ☐ Matthew 7:15-25 ☐ Romans 12:3-13 ☐ Philippians 1:9-11 ☐ Titus 3:14 ☐ James 2:14-26 ☐ Hebrews 13:15-16	**WE BEAR FRUIT IN HIM**
Thursday: ☐ 1 Cor 6:19 ☐	**Thursday:** ☐ Romans 8:1-30 ☐ Acts 11:15-16 ☐ Acts 2:38	**Thursday:** ☐ Isaiah 32:14-15 ☐ Acts 2:38-39 ☐ Romans 8:9-11 ☐ 1 Corinthians 12:12-14 ☐ 2 Timothy 1:6-14 ☐ 1 Peter 3:8-22 ☐	**HOLY SPIRIT ABIDES IN US**
Friday: ☐ 1 John 4:7-12 ☐	**Friday:** ☐ Mark 12:28-33 ☐ 1 John 4:13-21 ☐ 1 John 5:1-5	**Friday:** ☐ Deuteronomy 7:9-15 ☐ John 14:23-24 ☐ 1 Corinthians 13:1-13 ☐ 1 Peter 4:7-11 ☐ 1 John 2:3-17 ☐ ☐	**LOVE: EVIDENCE OF GOD IN US**

Unless we form the habit of going to the Bible in bright moments as well as in trouble, we cannot fully respond to its consolations because we lack equilibrium between light and darkness.
-Helen Keller

God's Word, "A Lost Book"

There was a time when the Bible was chained to the pulpit…only for the clergy! Common men, women and children could only know God's Word through the filtered minds of human priests. The message of God was corrupted by the traditions of men. In many homes, the Bible is just as lost under layers of dust, rarely read! The Book of God can be lost!

The Bible story of King Josiah encourages us to respect and read God's book (2 Kings 22 NIV). Josiah was only 8 years old when he became king. The Bible says "he did not turn away from doing what was right". When he was 16 years old he began worshipping God. As a young 20-year old adult, he began removing the idols and cleansed the land by breaking down the idol altars. When he was 26 years old he sent Hilkiah the High Priest and Shaphan his secretary to cleanse the temple of God.

Hezekiah reported back *"I have found the Book of the Law in the temple of the Lord"!* When the young king heard this he "*tore his clothes*" as a sign of genuine repentance and respect. He then charged the High Priest to "*read what is written in the book*" and to proclaim it to all the people.

The message from the lost book was clear: *"Great is the Lord's anger that burns against us because those who have gone before us have not obeyed the words of this book; they have not acted in accordance with all that is written there concerning us."* In addition, due to such neglect God's anger was to *"burn against this place and will not be quenched"*.

Josiah had a good heart, and was humble. He sincerely wanted to reverence and respect the Lord's will. As a result, the disaster God intended to bring upon the land due to their neglect of His Book, was averted during Josiah's lifetime.

Then Josiah gathered everyone in Judah together and read to them the Book of God's Promise that had been found in the temple. And the king in turn made a promise to God to walk in His ways and keep His commandments with all his heart and all His soul. And he asked everyone else to promise as well. So, for as long as Josiah was king the people did not stop following God.

Don't let your Bible become a "lost book"! These are the very words of God to be read, understood and obeyed. Disaster will come upon us if we turn from The Book. Continue to read even on days when you seem too busy, or do not feel like it. Like any "habit", reading the Bible will depend on your repetitive practice of doing it over and over and over….

**"What is more pleasing to the LORD:
your burnt offerings and sacrifices or your obedience to his voice?
Listen! Obedience is better than sacrifice,
and submission is better than offering the fat of rams.
Rebellion is as sinful as witchcraft, and stubbornness as bad as worshiping idols."
(1 Samuel 15:21-22)**

3rd Bible Reading Marathon

WEEK 6: [Dates:..........................] **PROMISES OF GOD:** *Transformed in Christ*

INSIDE TRACK	MIDDLE LANES	FAST TRACK	
Monday:	**Monday:**	**Monday:**	**TRANSFORMED INTO HIS GLORY**
☐ 2 Cor 3:18	☐ Galatians 2:19-21	☐ Romans 8:1-30	
☐ Gen 1:26-28	☐ John 1:1-15	☐ Ephesians 4:20-32	
	☐ Romans 1:16-17	☐ Romans 12:1-2	
		☐ I John 3:1-3	
		☐ I Timothy 4:12	
Tuesday:	**Tuesday:**	**Tuesday:**	**A NEW CREATION**
☐ 2 Cor 5:17	☐ 2 Peter 1:3-4	☐ Romans 6:1-14	
☐ Ezek 11:19-20	☐ Romans 6:1-4	☐ John 3:1-21	
	☐ Galatians 6:1-18	☐ Isaiah 43:18-19	
		☐ 1 Peter 3:18-22	
		☐ John 6:55-59	
Wednesday:	**Wednesday:**	**Wednesday:**	**PUT OFF SIN**
☐ Heb 4:15-16	☐ Romans 13:1-10	☐ Ephesians 2:1-22	
☐	☐ Titus 3:1-8	☐ 2 Peter 2:4-9	
	☐ Hebrews 12:1-2	☐ I Peter 4:1-11	
		☐ Galatians 5:19-21	
		☐ Psalm 51:1-4	
		☐ Romans 6:15-18	
Thursday:	**Thursday:**	**Thursday:**	**PUT ON CHRIST**
☐ Col 3:9-10	☐ Rev 3:1-6 & 15-16	☐ John 14:15-21	
☐	☐ John 17:20-26	☐ Galatians 3:23-29	
	☐ Romans 13:11-14	☐ Colossians 1:24-29	
		☐ Philippians 2:1-18	
		☐ Romans 8:9-11	
		☐ Ephesians 3:14-18	
		☐ I John 3:24	
Friday:	**Friday:**	**Friday:**	**A MINISTRY OF RECONCILIATION**
☐ 2 Cor 5:18-21	☐ Ephesians 2:14-22	☐ Acts 9:26-30	
☐	☐ Colossians 1:19-23	☐ Luke 15:1-32	
	☐ John 17:20-23	☐ Hebrews 12:14	
		☐ Matthew 18:15-20	
		☐ Matthew 5:21-26	

The Bible is the rock on which this Republic rests.

-Andrew Jackson

3rd Bible Reading Marathon

WEEK 7: [Dates:..........................] **PROMISES OF GOD:** *God Gives us Power!*

INSIDE TRACK	MIDDLE LANES	FAST TRACK	
Monday:	**Monday:**	**Monday:**	**GOD'S FELLOW-WORKERS**
☐ John 14:12	☐ 2 Peter 3:8-13	☐ Genesis 1:1-31	
	☐ 2 Thessalonians 3:1-18	☐ Proverbs 3:1-35	
	☐ Philippians 3:1-21	☐ Deuteronomy 1:1-46	
		☐ Acts 14:1-28	
		☐ Galatians 3:1-29	
Tuesday:	**Tuesday:**	**Tuesday:**	**STRONG "IN THE LORD"**
☐ Ephesians 6:10	☐ Psalm 139:1-24	☐ Acts 9:1-43	
	☐ 2 Corinthians 3:1-18	☐ Luke 1:1-80	
	☐ John 15:1-8	☐ Mark 1:1-45	
		☐ Isaiah 5:1-30	
		☐ Acts 2:1-47	
Wednesday:	**Wednesday:**	**Wednesday:**	**STRONGER THAN SATAN**
☐ 2 Cor 10:4	☐ Hebrews 3:1-19	☐ Proverbs 1:1-33	
	☐ 1 Corinthians 13:1-13	☐ Daniel 5:1-31	
	☐ Zechariah 6:1-15	☐ Lamentations 5:1-22	
		☐ Jeremiah 5:1-31	
		☐ Psalms 127:1-24	
Thursday:	**Thursday:**	**Thursday:**	**THE POWER OF FAITH**
☐ Matthew 17:20	☐ Exodus 3:1-14	☐ Ecclesiastes 3:1-22	
	☐ Revelation 5:1-14	☐ 2 Timothy 4:1-22	
	☐ Micah 6:1-16	☐ Colossians 3:1-25	
		☐ Ephesians 4:1-32	
		☐ Luke 9:1-62	
Friday:	**Friday:**	**Friday:**	**POWER OF GOD'S WORD**
☐ 2 Tim 3:14-16	☐ James 3:1-18	☐ Job 3:1-26	
	☐ 2 Peter 3:1-18	☐ Romans 3:1-31	
	☐ Ecclesiastes 3:1-22	☐ Acts 15:1-41	
		☐ John 1:1-51	
		☐ Matthew 1:1-25	

"Take all that you can of this book upon reason, and the balance on faith, and you will live and die a happier man. (When a skeptic expressed surprise to see him reading a Bible)"

-Abraham Lincoln

3rd Bible Reading Marathon

WEEK 8: [Dates:..........................]	PROMISES OF GOD: *Freedom in Christ*

INSIDE TRACK	MIDDLE LANES	FAST TRACK	
Monday: ☐ John 8:31-32 ☐	**Monday:** ☐ 2 Kings 5:1-14 ☐ John 8:31-47 ☐	**Monday:** ☐ Romans 8:18-21 ☐ 2 Corinthians 3:17-18 ☐ John 17:13-17 ☐ Psalm 119:105 ☐ Isaiah 55:8-11 ☐ Psalm 119:159-160 ☐	**TRUTH SETS US FREE**
Tuesday: ☐ Romans 6:18 ☐	**Tuesday:** ☐ Acts 2 ☐ Romans 6 ☐ Acts 10:43	**Tuesday:** ☐ Acts 13:38-39 ☐ Romans 3:21-26 ☐ Ephesians 3:12 ☐ Colossians 1:21-23 ☐ 1 Peter 2:16-17 ☐ Ezekiel 36:25-26 ☐ Hebrews 10:1-18	**FREEDOM FROM SIN**
Wednesday: ☐ 2 Cor 10:4 ☐	**Wednesday:** ☐ Psalm 18 ☐ Ephesians 6:10-20 ☐	**Wednesday:** ☐ 1 Timothy 1:18-20 ☐ 1 Timothy 6:11-16 ☐ James 4:7-10 ☐ Leviticus 26:3-13 ☐ Romans 8:31-39 ☐ 2 Timothy 4:1-8 ☐	**FREE TO FIGHT**
Thursday: ☐ Ephesians 2:10 ☐	**Thursday:** ☐ Matthew 5:13-16 ☐ James 2:14-26 ☐	**Thursday:** ☐ 2 Timothy 3:16-17 ☐ Colossians 3:23-24 ☐ Titus 3:1-2 ☐ Galatians 6:1-10 ☐ Proverbs 3:27-28 ☐ 1 Peter 3:13-17 ☐	**TO DO GOOD WORKS**
Friday: ☐ Romans 8:28 ☐	**Friday:** ☐ Romans 8 ☐ Esther 4 ☐	**Friday:** ☐ 1 Corinthians 3:1-9 ☐ 2 Corinthians 6:1-2 ☐ 2 Chronicles 7:14-15 ☐ Psalm 146 ☐ Philippians 2:12-13 ☐ ☐	**WORKING TOGETHER WITH GOD**

"But for this book we could not know right from wrong."

– Abraham Lincoln

3rd Bible Reading Marathon

WEEK 9: [Dates:………………………..] **PROMISES OF GOD:** *Jesus, is the Only Way*

INSIDE TRACK	MIDDLE LANES	FAST TRACK	
Monday:	**Monday:**	**Monday:**	**JESUS ONLY!**
☐ John 14:6	☐ Isaiah 40: 1-24	☐ Proverbs 14: 12	
☐	☐	☐ Proverbs 16: 25	
	☐	☐ Acts 22: 1-25	
		☐	
		☐	
		☐	
		☐	
Tuesday:	**Tuesday:**	**Tuesday:**	**JESUS: ONLY MEDIATOR**
☐ 1 Timothy 2:5	☐ Hebrews 8: 1-13	☐ Galatians 3: 1-29	
☐	☐ Hebrews 9: 11-28	☐ Hebrews 12: 18-28	
	☐	☐	
		☐	
		☐	
		☐	
		☐	
Wednesday:	**Wednesday:**	**Wednesday:**	**JESUS: ONE BODY, ONE CHURCH**
☐ Colossians 1:18	☐ Romans 12: 1-8	☐ 1 Corinthians 10: 14-17	
☐	☐ 1 Corinthians 12: 12-30	☐ Ephesians 2: 11-19	
	☐	☐ Ephesians 3: 1-6	
		☐ Ephesians 4: 1-16	
		☐	
		☐	
		☐	
Thursday:	**Thursday:**	**Thursday:**	**JESUS: THE ONLY RECONCILER**
☐ Col 1:19-20	☐ 2 Corinthians 5: 11-21	☐ Isaiah 9: 1-7	
☐	☐ Colossians 1: 15-23	☐ Psalm 27: 7-14	
	☐	☐ Romans 5: 1-11	
		☐ Matthew 4: 12-25	
		☐	
		☐	
		☐	
Friday:	**Friday:**	**Friday:**	**JESUS: ONLY WAY OF SALVATION**
☐ John 1:29	☐ John 10: 1-14	☐ Matthew 7: 13-27	
☐	☐ Acts 4: 1-12	☐ John 14: 1-18	
	☐	☐ Ephesians 2: 1-10	
		☐	
		☐	
		☐	
		☐	

"The Holy Scriptures are our letters from home."
- Augustine of Hippo

3rd Bible Reading Marathon

WEEK 10: [Dates:..........................] **PROMISES OF GOD:** *Strength When We are Weak!*

INSIDE TRACK	MIDDLE LANES	FAST TRACK	
Monday: ☐ Isaiah 40:29-31 ☐	**Monday:** ☐ Psalms 23:1-6 ☐ Isaiah 63:7-14 ☐	**Monday:** ☐ Exodus 20:8-11 ☐ 1 Kings 8:56-61 ☐ Jeremiah 31:23-26 ☐ Mark 6:30-34 ☐ Galatians 6:9 ☐ 2 Thessalonians 3:11-13 ☐ Hebrews 12:1-3	**REST WHEN WE ARE WEARY**
Tuesday: ☐ Matt 11:28-29 ☐	**Tuesday:** ☐ Hebrews 3:7-19 ☐ Hebrews 4:1-16 ☐	**Tuesday:** ☐ Psalms 37:1-11 ☐ John 3:14-17 ☐ John 4:13-14 ☐ Revelation 22:17 ☐ John 14:1-4 ☐ 2 Timothy 4:7-8 ☐ James 1:12	**REST FOR OUR SOULS**
Wednesday: ☐ Psalms 27:1 ☐	**Wednesday:** ☐ Exodus 4:1-17 ☐ 2 Timothy 1:7-10 ☐ Psalms 46:1-3, 10-11	**Wednesday:** ☐ Psalms 37:1-11 ☐ John 3:14-17 ☐ John 4:13-14 ☐ Revelation 22:17 ☐ John 14:1-4 ☐ 2 Timothy 4:7-8 ☐ James 1:12	**HELP TO OVERCOME FEAR**
Thursday: ☐ Psalms 119:28 ☐	**Thursday:** ☐ Psalms 121:1-8 ☐ Isaiah 61:1-3 ☐ Luke 4:16-21	**Thursday:** ☐ Isaiah 53:4-6 ☐ Isaiah 66:12-13 ☐ Matthew 5:4 ☐ John 11:23-27 ☐ 2 Corinthians 1:3-7 ☐ 2 Cor 4:16-18 & 12:7-10 ☐ 1 Thessalonians 4:13-18	**COMFORT IN SORROW**
Friday: ☐ Phil 4:13 ☐	**Friday:** ☐ Matthew 19:16-30 ☐ 2 Corinthians 1:18-22 ☐	**Friday:** ☐ Job 19:23-27 ☐ Romans 4:18-21 ☐ Romans 8:28-39 ☐ Ephesians 2:3-10 ☐ 2 Peter 1:3-4 ☐ ☐	**ALL THINGS ARE POSSIBLE**

"Reading the Bible will help you get to know the word, but it's when you put it down and live your life that you get to know the author."

-Steve Maraboli,

3rd Bible Reading Marathon

WEEK 11: [Dates:……………………..] **PROMISES OF GOD:** *If We seek, We will Find*

INSIDE TRACK	MIDDLE LANES	FAST TRACK	
Monday: ☐ Matthew 7:7-8 ☐ Amos 5:4	**Monday:** ☐ I Chron. 16:10-12 ☐ Luke 13:6-9 ☐ John 12:20-36	**Monday:** ☐ Psalms 10:4 ☐ Psalms 27:4 ☐ Psalms 63:1 ☐ Isaiah 55:6 ☐ John 5:30 ☐ Jeremiah 29:11-13 ☐	**SEEK GOD FIRST**
Tuesday: ☐ Matthew 6:31 ☐ Psalms 27:8	**Tuesday:** ☐ Psalms 63:1-11 ☐ Psalms 42:1-11 ☐ Psalms 143:1-12	**Tuesday:** ☐ 2 Chron. 22:19 ☐ 2 Chron. 19:3 ☐ Ezra 4:2 ☐ Ezra 6:21 ☐ Amos 5:6 ☐ Matthew 6:32-33 ☐	**SEEK NOT THINGS OF WORLD**
Wednesday: ☐ Matthew 6:33 ☐ Deut 4:29	**Wednesday:** ☐ Luke 15:1-7 ☐ Luke 15:8-10 ☐ Luke 15:11-32	**Wednesday:** ☐ Isaiah 51:1 ☐ Jer. 45:5 ☐ Zephaniah 2:3 ☐ John 7:33-34 ☐ Hebrews 13:13-15 ☐ Colossians 3:1 ☐	**SEEK THE KINGDOM OF HEAVEN**
Thursday: ☐ 1 Peter 3:10-11 ☐ Proverbs 8:17	**Thursday:** ☐ Matthew 13:44-50 ☐ Luke 11:5-10 ☐ Acts 8:26-39	**Thursday:** ☐ I Chron. 28:9 ☐ Psalms 34:10 ☐ Jer. 29:13-14 ☐ Romans 9:30-32 ☐ Hebrews 11:6 ☐ Acts 17:26-27 ☐	**SEEK PEACE WITH OTHERS**
Friday: ☐ Prov 2:10-11 ☐ Proverbs 28:5	**Friday:** ☐ Jer. 29:10-14 ☐ John 7:32-36 ☐ Luke 19:9-10	**Friday:** ☐ 2 Chron. 7:14 ☐ Isaiah 8:19 ☐ Isaiah 40:31 ☐ Ezekiel 34:16 ☐ Romans 2:5-7 ☐ Luke 19:9-10 ☐	**SEEK WISDOM**

"A Bible that's falling apart usually belongs to someone who isn't."

– Charles H. Spurgeon

3rd Bible Reading Marathon

WEEK 12: [Dates:..............................] **PROMISES OF GOD:** *Being Fruitful*

INSIDE TRACK

Monday:
- [ ] Gal. 5:22-26
- [ ]

Tuesday:
- [ ] John 15:2-8
- [ ]

Wednesday:
- [ ] Rom. 6:12-13
- [ ]

Thursday:
- [ ] 2 Peter 1:5-9
- [ ]

Friday:
- [ ] Matthew 21:19
- [ ]

MIDDLE LANES

Monday:
- [ ] Genesis 6:8-22
- [ ] Genesis 7:1-5
- [ ] Genesis 9:1-17

Tuesday:
- [ ] Genesis 4:15-52
- [ ]
- [ ]

Wednesday:
- [ ] Acts 9:1-31
- [ ]
- [ ]

Thursday:
- [ ] Acts 2:22-41
- [ ]
- [ ]

Friday:
- [ ] Matthew 13:24-50
- [ ]
- [ ]

FAST TRACK

Monday:
- [ ] Matthew 7L15-20
- [ ] 2 Peter 1:5-7
- [ ] Colossians 1:10-12
- [ ] Colossians 3:12-15
- [ ] 2 Thessalonians 1:11
- [ ] 1 Timothy 1:16
- [ ] Matthew 6:23

Tuesday:
- [ ] John 15:5-16
- [ ] Titus 3:14
- [ ] Hebrews 13:15
- [ ] Philippians 1:9-11
- [ ] Ephesians 6:1-4
- [ ]
- [ ]

Wednesday:
- [ ] Romans 6:1-28
- [ ] Romans 12:1-2
- [ ] Colossians 3:5
- [ ] Galatians 5:19-21
- [ ] John 14:15
- [ ]
- [ ]

Thursday:
- [ ] 1 John 1:5-10
- [ ] Galatians 5:22-23
- [ ] Romans 7:4-6
- [ ] Ephesians 2:8-10
- [ ] James 3:18
- [ ]
- [ ]

Friday:
- [ ] Ephesians 5:11-12
- [ ] Proverbs 10:4
- [ ] James 5:7-9
- [ ] 1 Timothy 6:17-19
- [ ] Revelation 21:8
- [ ]
- [ ]

THE RIGHT KIND OF FRUIT

MUST ABIDE IN CHRIST TO PRODUCE FRUIT

YIELD (SUBMIT) TO GOD

BEARING FRUIT TAKES EFFORT

FRUITLESSNESS EQUALS DEATH

"You Christians look after a document containing enough dynamite to blow all civilisation to pieces, turn the world upside down and bring peace to a battle-torn planet. But you treat it as though it is nothing more than a piece of literature." — Mahatma Gandhi

3rd Bible Reading Marathon

WEEK 13: [Dates:..........................]   **PROMISES OF GOD:**   *God's Love*

INSIDE TRACK	MIDDLE LANES	FAST TRACK	
Monday:	**Monday:**	**Monday:**	**HOW GREAT IS HIS LOVE**
☐ Ephesians 2:4-7	☐ John 19:1-30	☐ Jeremiah 1:4, 5	
☐ John 3:16	☐ 2 Peter 3:9	☐ Zephaniah 3:14-18	
	☐	☐ John 17:20-26	
		☐ Romans 8:37-39	
		☐ Galatians 2:17-21	
		☐ 1 John 4:8-10	
		☐	
Tuesday:	**Tuesday:**	**Tuesday:**	**GOD LOVED HIS SON**
☐ John 3:34-36	☐ Isaiah 53:1-11	☐ Isaiah 9:6, 7	
☐ Mark 1:9-11	☐ Mark 12:1-12	☐ Luke 2:41-52	
	☐	☐ John 1:1-18	
		☐ John 5:10-23	
		☐ Titus 2:11-14	
		☐ Revelation 3:20, 21	
		☐	
Wednesday:	**Wednesday:**	**Wednesday:**	**GOD LOVES THE WORLD**
☐ Titus 1:2	☐ Proverbs 3:11, 12	☐ Psalms 91:1-16	
☐ 1 Peter 5:6, 7	☐ Matthew 27:27-54	☐ Matthew 23:37-39	
	☐ 1 John 4:7-12	☐ John 13:34, 35	
		☐ John 16:25-28	
		☐ 1 John 3:1-3	
		☐	
		☐	
Thursday:	**Thursday:**	**Thursday:**	**GOD LOVES SINNERS**
☐ Romans 5:8	☐ John 8:1-11	☐ Matthew 5:43-48	
☐ Acts 2:36-38	☐ Luke 6:27-36	☐ Romans 3:21-31	
	☐	☐ Romans 5:1-10	
		☐ 1 John 1:8-10	
		☐	
		☐	
		☐	
Friday:	**Friday:**	**Friday:**	**GOD'S LOVE IS EVERLASTING**
☐ Jeremiah 31:3	☐ Ephesians 3:14-21	☐ Psalms 118:1-29	
☐ Psalms 136:26	☐ Hebrews 13:5	☐ John 14:1-4	
	☐ Psalms 100:1-5	☐ John 14:22, 23	
		☐ Romans 8:31-39	
		☐	
		☐	
		☐	

"The primary purpose of reading the Bible is not to know the Bible but to know God."

–James Merritt

3rd Bible Reading Marathon

WEEK 14: [Dates:..........................]   **PROMISES OF GOD:** *Our Love in Practice*

INSIDE TRACK	MIDDLE LANES	FAST TRACK	
Monday: ☐ Mark 12:30 ☐ Deut 6:4-6	**Monday:** ☐ James 4:4-10 ☐ Psalm 96:1-13 ☐ John 20:15-17	**Monday:** ☐ Acts 13:22 ☐ 1 Samuel 17:45-46 ☐ 1 Samuel 26:5-11 ☐ 2 Samuel 22:29-33 ☐ 1 Kings 2:1-3 ☐ 1 Kings 11:4	**THE FIRST COMMANDMENT**
Tuesday: ☐ Matt 22:38-40	**Tuesday:** ☐ 1 John 3:11-24 ☐ Luke 10:25-37	**Tuesday:** ☐ 1 Samuel 18:1-4 ☐ 1 Samuel 20:1-42 ☐ 2 Samuel 9:1-8	**THE SECOND COMMANDMENT**
Wednesday: ☐ 1 John 4:21	**Wednesday:** ☐ 1 Peter 1:22-23 ☐ 1 Peter 4:8-11 ☐ Romans 12:6-10	**Wednesday:** ☐ Philippians 1:3-11 ☐ Galatians 6:1-3 ☐ Romans 14:13-23 ☐ Romans 15:1-7 ☐ 1 Timothy 1:5	**HOW TO LOVE MY BROTHER**
Thursday: ☐ Matt 5:43-47	**Thursday:** ☐ Romans 12:14, 17-21 ☐ Jude 17-22 ☐ James 5:19-21	**Thursday:** ☐ Luke 23:33-49 ☐ Romans 5:1-11 ☐ 1 Peter 2:21-25 ☐ 1 Peter 3:8-17	**LOVE YOUR ENEMIES**
Friday: ☐ John 13:34-35	**Friday:** ☐ 1 John 5:1-3 ☐ 1 John 3:7-10, 14 ☐ 1 John 2:7-11	**Friday:** ☐ 2 Corinthians 9:3, 11-15 ☐ Philemon 4-7 ☐ 1 Corinthians 13:1-13	**LOVE, PROOF OF DISCIPLESHIP**

A little girl repeating the Twenty-Third Psalm said it this way:

"The Lord is my Shepherd, that's all I want"

JUST KEEP IN MIND!

AS YOU READ...

Memory research indicates that it takes 10-12 weeks to form a new habit. We are the products of our habits. That's why we prepared the Bible Reading Marathon. It has been designed to help you form the "good habit" of reading God's Word, the Bible. You have now been involved in the program for thirteen weeks...the habit must be forming! Now, you probably look forward to "the habit", and miss it if you forget to read, or otherwise are distracted from your routine. That's good! But remember, your Bible reading habit is actually a process to much more important goals:

So, you are half-way through the Marathon. Remember, *everyone who finishes* is a winner!

WHY WE READ THE BIBLE...

TO KNOW GOD:

Our God is not far away nor uncaring! Through Jesus He *became flesh and dwelt among us, and we beheld His glory, the glory as of the only begotten of the Father, full of grace and truth (John 1:14 NKJV).* Our God made the world and everything in it...thus, we *"should seek the Lord, in the hope that ..(we).. might grope for Him and find Him, though He is not far from each one of us;" (Acts 17:27 NKJV).* We can all "know God" from the least to the greatest!

TO KNOW JESUS, HIS SON:

Jesus was the express image of His father. The Bible says, *Who, being in very nature of God, did not consider equality with God something to be used to his own advantage; rather, he made himself nothing by taking the very nature of a servant, being made in human likeness. (*Philippians 2:6-7 NIV). Jesus expressed the exclusive way to know God: *"I am the way and the truth and the life. No one comes to the Father except through me. (*John 14:6 NIV).

TO KNOW OURSELVES:

Jesus taught that the heart that responds to God is like a fertile, well-tilled field (Luke 8:11-18 NKJV) which receives *"the seed"* which is *"the word of God."* As you read, how receptive is your heart to God's message? David, a man after God's heart, posed the question like this: "..you (God) probe my heart, though you examine me at night and test me" (Psalms 17:3 NIV). He wanted God to "search him" and know his heart (Psalms 139).

TO KNOW GOD'S PLAN FOR US:

God's plan is to set us free from sin and make us disciples of His Son, Jesus. *"Sanctify them by Your truth. Your word is truth" (*John 17:17 NKJV). Paul wrote to the Thessalonian church *"...when you received the word of God which you heard from us, you welcomed it not as the word of men, but as it is in truth, the word of God, which also effectively works in you who believe." (1 Thessalonians 2:13)* God *"desires all men to be saved and to come to the knowledge of the truth."* (1 Timothy 2:4 NKJV).

Continue in prayer, study, and perseverance as you race toward the finish line. Be a winner! More than that, enjoy the wonderful benefits of joy, enlightenment, and spiritual growth as you read. God's Word is truly a "lamp unto our feet and a light unto our pathways"!

3rd Bible Reading Marathon

WEEK 15: [Dates:..........................] **PROMISES OF GOD:** *Grace for Good Works*

INSIDE TRACK

Monday:
- [ ] 2 Cor 9:8

Tuesday:
- [ ] Rom 9:31-32

Wednesday:
- [ ] 1 Cor 3:11-14

Thursday:
- [ ] Ephesians 2:10

Friday:
- [ ] Matthew 5:16

MIDDLE LANES

Monday:
- [ ] 2 Corinthians 12:7-10
- [ ] Genesis 28:10-22
- [ ] 1 Peter 2:1-25

Tuesday:
- [ ] 2 Peter 3:1-18
- [ ] James 4:1-12
- [ ] Acts 16:22-40

Wednesday:
- [ ] Revelation 2:8-11
- [ ] Matthew 25:31-46
- [ ] John 15:1-11

Thursday:
- [ ] 1 Corinthians 16:1-4
- [ ] 2 Corinthians 8:1-9
- [ ] 2 Corinthians 9:6-15

Friday:
- [ ] 1 Corinthians 6:1-20
- [ ] Judges 16:25-30

FAST TRACK

Monday:
- [ ] Isaiah 41:8-13
- [ ] Hebrews 13:5-6
- [ ] Philippians 4:10-14
- [ ] Malachi 3:8-10
- [ ] Genesis 1:26-28

Tuesday:
- [ ] Isaiah 55:1-3
- [ ] John 14:1-4; 27-31
- [ ] Romans 8:24-30
- [ ] Psalms 103:1-18

Wednesday:
- [ ] Revelation 20:11-15
- [ ] Revelation 14:13
- [ ] Titus 2:14
- [ ] Colossians 3:17-24
- [ ] Ephesians 6:5-9
- [ ] 1 Corinthians 3:5-17

Thursday:
- [ ] Ephesians 2:4-10
- [ ] Matthew 5:13-16
- [ ] 1 Peter 2:7-12
- [ ] James 2:14-26
- [ ] Luke 21:1-4

Friday:
- [ ] Job 12:7-10
- [ ] Psalms 34:1-22
- [ ] 1 Corinthians 3:16
- [ ] Psalms 19:1-14
- [ ] 1 Corinthians 10:23-33

GOD IS ABLE TO HELP

GOD IS FOR US

GOOD WORKS ARE REWARDED

CREATED FOR GOOD WORKS

GOOD WORKS GLORIFY GOD

"The Bible shows how the world progresses. It begins with a garden, but ends with a holy city"

– Phillip Brooks

3rd Bible Reading Marathon

WEEK 16: [Dates:............................] **PROMISES OF GOD:** *God Will Give us Rest*

INSIDE TRACK	MIDDLE LANES	FAST TRACK	
Monday:	**Monday:**	**Monday:**	**CHRIST GIVES US REST**
☐ Matt 11:28-30	☐ Isaiah 53:4-12	☐ Hebrews 4:1-15	
☐	☐ Matthew 8:16-17	☐ Matthew 9:35-36	
	☐ John 19:17-18	☐ Matthew 14:14-21	
		☐ Matthew 15:32	
		☐ Matthew 20:34	
		☐ Luke 7:13	
		☐ John 11:35	
Tuesday:	**Tuesday:**	**Tuesday:**	**NO REST FOR THE WICKED**
☐ Isaiah 57:19-21	☐ 2 Timothy 3:1-9	☐ 2 Chronicles 15:5	
☐	☐ Lamentations 5:5	☐ Isaiah 48:22	
	☐ Deuteronomy 28:15	☐ Isaiah 59:8	
		☐ Deuteronomy 28:15-68	
		☐	
		☐	
		☐	
Wednesday:	**Wednesday:**	**Wednesday:**	**WAIT ON THE LORD**
☐ Psalms 37:7-9	☐ Psalms 40:1-17	☐ Isaiah 25:9	
☐	☐ Psalms 130:6	☐ Genesis 49:18	
	☐	☐ Psalms 33:1-20	
		☐ Isaiah 26:8	
		☐ Isaiah 33:2	
		☐ Luke 2:25-32	
		☐	
Thursday:	**Thursday:**	**Thursday:**	**SABBATH DAY & SABBATH REST**
☐ Hebrews 4:9-11	☐ Exodus 33:14	☐ 2 Thessalonians 1:1-7	
☐ Matthew 11:29	☐ Psalms 55:6	☐ Isaiah 57:2	
	☐ Isaiah 28:12	☐ Exodus 23:12	
		☐ Exodus 20:8	
		☐ Isaiah 58:13	
		☐ Isaiah 56:2	
		☐ Matthew 12:12	
Friday:	**Friday:**	**Friday:**	**ETERNAL REST**
☐ Rev 14:13	☐ Luke 14:12-14	☐ 2 Timothy 4:1-8	
☐	☐ Proverbs 11:31	☐ Matthew 25:23	
	☐ Proverbs 13:21	☐ Ephesians 6:8	
		☐ Acts 20:32	
		☐ Acts 26:18	
		☐ Eph 1:11	
		☐ Isaiah 35:4	

"The Bible is the truest utterance that ever came by alphabetic letters from the soul of man, through which, as through a window divinely opened, all men can look into the stillness of eternity, and discern in glimpses their far-distant, long-forgotten home" - Thomas Carlyle

3rd Bible Reading Marathon

WEEK 17: [Dates:............................] **PROMISES OF GOD:** *Not Overcome by Temptations*

INSIDE TRACK	MIDDLE LANES	FAST TRACK	
Monday:	**Monday:**	**Monday:**	**WE ARE TEMPTED**
☐ James 1:13-14	☐ Matthew 26:40-41	☐ James 1:1-27	
☐	☐ Luke 22:39-46	☐ I Peter 5:8-9	
	☐ Ephesians 4:17-32	☐ Acts 14:21-22	
		☐	
		☐	
		☐	
Tuesday:	**Tuesday:**	**Tuesday:**	**CAUGHT IN A SNARE**
☐ 1 Cor 10:12-13	☐ Hebrews 2:18	☐ I Timothy 6:3-21	
☐	☐ I Corinthians 15: 33-34	☐ Titus 1:10-16	
	☐ Galatians 6:7-10	☐ II John	
		☐ Luke 17:1-4	
		☐	
		☐	
Wednesday:	**Wednesday:**	**Wednesday:**	**FACING TEMPTATIONS**
☐ Job 1:9-12	☐ Proverbs 1:10-15	☐ Ephesians 6:10-20	
☐	☐ II Timothy 2:22-25	☐ Luke 21:29-36	
	☐ Luke 4:1-13	☐ Hebrews 12:1-4	
		☐ Romans 6:12-23	
		☐ Matthew 6:13	
		☐	
Thursday:	**Thursday:**	**Thursday:**	**RESCUED BY GOD**
☐ 2 Peter 2:4-9	☐ Hebrews 4:14-16	☐ James 4:7-10	
☐	☐ Psalms 94:12-15	☐ Isaiah 50:7-9	
	☐ Isaiah 41:10-13	☐ Psalms 34:1-22	
		☐ Romans 8:31-35	
		☐ 2 Chronicles 16:8-9	
		☐	
Friday:	**Friday:**	**Friday:**	**SOURCES OF HOPE**
☐ Heb 10:23-25	☐ Galatians 5:13-26	☐ Psalms 37:1-40	
☐	☐ Joshua 1:9	☐ Colossians 2:1-5	
	☐ Proverbs 13:9	☐ Ephesians 5:15-20	

"The secret of my success? It is simple. It is found in the Bible,
"In all thy ways acknowledge Him and He shall direct thy paths"
-George Washington Carver

3rd Bible Reading Marathon

WEEK 18: [Dates:...........................] **PROMISES OF GOD:** *Unity in Christ*

INSIDE TRACK	MIDDLE LANES	FAST TRACK	
Monday: ☐ Ephesians 4:1-4	**Monday:** ☐ Matthew 12:22-28 ☐ Acts 15:36-41 ☐ Genesis 2:19-25	**Monday:** ☐ Jude 12-23 ☐ 1 Corinthians 1:10-17 ☐ Romans 16:17-19 ☐ Colossians 2:13-19 ☐ Titus 3:9-11 ☐ John 17:20-23	**BECOMING ONE**
Tuesday: ☐ Col 1:21-25	**Tuesday:** ☐ Nehemiah 4:1-23 ☐ Matthew 16:13-20 ☐ Acts 2:42-47	**Tuesday:** ☐ 1 Corinthians 12:1-30 ☐ Colossians 3:11-17 ☐ Psalms 133:1-3 ☐ Ephesians 1:15-23 ☐ Ephesians 2:11-22	**ONE BODY, THE CHURCH**
Wednesday: ☐ Eph 1:19-23	**Wednesday:** ☐ John 20:24-31 ☐ Luke 24:1-8 ☐ Luke 12:35-48	**Wednesday:** ☐ Romans 10:1-13 ☐ Philippians 2:1-11 ☐ Revelation 4:1-11 ☐ 1 Corinthians 15:3-7 ☐ 1 Timothy 1:3; 12-17 ☐ Romans 1:1-7 ☐ Revelation 22:12-21	**ONE LORD**
Thursday: ☐ Jude 3	**Thursday:** ☐ Acts 6:1-7 ☐ Acts 13:6-12	**Thursday:** ☐ Galatians 1:6-17 ☐ 2 Peter 1:12-21 ☐ 2 John 1-13 ☐ Acts 14:19-28 ☐ 1 Thessalonians 2:1-13 ☐ 2 Timothy 4:6-8	**ONE FAITH**
Friday: ☐ 1 Peter 3:18-21	**Friday:** ☐ Acts 8:26-40 ☐ Acts 22:1-16 ☐ Matthew 3:1-17	**Friday:** ☐ Romans 6:1-14 ☐ Galatians 3:26-29 ☐ Titus 3:3-7 ☐ 1 Corinthians 12:12-13 ☐ Mark 16:15-20 ☐ Acts 2:29-41 ☐ Matthew 28:19-20	**ONE BAPTISM**

"The foundations of our society and our government rest so much on the teachings of the Bible that it would be difficult to support them if faith in these teachings would cease to be practically universal in our country" -Calvin Coolidge

3rd Bible Reading Marathon

WEEK 19: [Dates:............................] **PROMISES OF GOD:** *Blessed for Reading God's Word*

INSIDE TRACK	MIDDLE LANES	FAST TRACK	
Monday:	**Monday:**	**Monday:**	**THE LAW OF THE LORD**
☐ Psalms 19:7-11	☐ Hebrews 4: 12-16	☐ Psalms 119: 105-108	
☐	☐ Psalms 119: 18	☐ John 5: 36-43	
	☐ Job 23: 10-12	☐ Matt. 22: 29-33	
		☐ Matt. 4: 4-11	
		☐ Isaiah 55: 10-11	
		☐ James 1: 19-25	
		☐ II Thessalonians 2: 13-17	
Tuesday:	**Tuesday:**	**Tuesday:**	**DESIRE GOD'S WORD**
☐ 1 Peter 2:1-3	☐ II Timothy 2:14-19	☐ II Timothy 3:10-17	
☐	☐ I Peter 2: 1-3	☐ Romans 2: 6-8	
	☐ Joshua 1: 6-9	☐ John 6: 60-71	
		☐ John 1:1-18	
		☐ I John 2:3-4	
		☐	
		☐	
Wednesday:	**Wednesday:**	**Wednesday:**	**MEDITATE ON GOD'S WORD DAILY**
☐ Joshua 1:8	☐ Psalms 119: 1-3 / 14-19	☐ Nehemiah 8: 1-8	
☐	☐ Ephesians 6: 10-17	☐ I Timothy 4: 5-10	
	☐ I Timothy 3: 14-15	☐ John 6: 43-59	
		☐ Psalms 119: 17-20	
		☐ Acts 21: 38-39	
		☐	
		☐	
Thursday:	**Thursday:**	**Thursday:**	**CLEANSES OUR WAYS**
☐ Psa 119: 10-11	☐ I Timothy 3:16	☐ Romans 15:1-5	
☐	☐ I Peter 3: 18-22	☐ Isaiah 25: 1-5	
	☐ I John 5: 6-12	☐ Psalms 1: 1-6	
		☐ II Timothy 2: 1-13	
		☐ Matthew 24:32-35	
		☐	
		☐	
Friday:	**Friday:**	**Friday:**	**STUDY GOD'S WORD**
☐ I Tim 4: 11-16	☐ Romans 3: 1-4	☐ I John 2: 3-17	
☐	☐ I Corinthians 12: 1-11	☐ Colossians 3: 1-17	
	☐ John 15: 1-11	☐ I Timothy 2: 1-8	
		☐ Revelation 1: 1-7	

"After more than sixty years of almost daily reading of the Bible, I never fail to find it always new and marvelously in tune with the changing needs of every day"

-Cecil B. DeMille

3rd Bible Reading Marathon

WEEK 20: [Dates:..........................] **PROMISES OF GOD:** *Train a Child for long Life*

INSIDE TRACK	MIDDLE LANES	FAST TRACK	
Monday: ☐ Deut 6:1-3 ☐	**Monday:** ☐ Genesis 22:1-12 ☐ Proverbs 2:1-15 ☐ Proverbs 9:10	**Monday:** ☐ Luke 12:4&5 ☐ Acts 9:31 ☐ I Peter 3:13&14 ☐ Psalms 34:9-15 ☐ Revelation 14:6&7 ☐ 2 Corinthians 5:11-16 ☐ Philippians 2:12&13	**TO FEAR GOD** _____ _____ _____ _____ _____
Tuesday: ☐ Ephesians 6:1-3 ☐	**Tuesday:** ☐ Deuteronomy 4:39-40 ☐ Proverbs 3:1-2 ☐ Deuteronomy 11:8-21	**Tuesday:** ☐ Genesis 6:5-8 ☐ Genesis 22:1-18 ☐ Deuteronomy 5:32&33 ☐ Proverbs 10:27 ☐ ☐ ☐	**TO LIVE LONG ON THE EARTH** _____ _____ _____ _____ _____
Wednesday: ☐ 2 Tim 3:15-16 ☐	**Wednesday:** ☐ Psalms 119:1-16 ☐ John 1:1-4; 14 ☐ Psalms 1:1-6	**Wednesday:** ☐ Matthew 4:1-4 ☐ James 1:22-25 ☐ Psalms 119:105 ☐ Ephesians 6:10-18 ☐ Deuteronomy 11:8-25 ☐ ☐	**TO KNOW GOD'S WORD** _____ _____ _____ _____ _____
Thursday: ☐ Colossians 3:21 ☐	**Thursday:** ☐ Hebrews 12:5-11 ☐ Luke 2:41-52 ☐ Proverbs 23:13-15	**Thursday:** ☐ Ephesians 6:4 ☐ Proverbs 13:24 ☐ I Samuel 2:12-26 ☐ Proverbs 1:8-19 ☐ Proverbs 29:15-17 ☐ ☐	**DISCIPLINE WITH LOVE** _____ _____ _____ _____ _____
Friday: ☐ 2 Timothy 1:5 ☐	**Friday:** ☐ Proverbs 22:6 ☐ Deuteronomy 4:9 ☐ Matthew 28:16-20	**Friday:** ☐ Deuteronomy 6:6-9 ☐ 2 Timothy 1:5 ☐ Deuteronomy 6:20-25 ☐ Isaiah 38:19 ☐ Acts 17:22-28 ☐ ☐	**PASS IT ON!** _____ _____ _____ _____ _____

"The more profoundly we study this wonderful Book (the Bible), and the more closely we observe its divine precepts the better citizens we will become and the higher will be our destiny as a nation"

-William McKinley

3rd Bible Reading Marathon

WEEK 21: [Dates:..........................] **PROMISES OF GOD:** Our *Prayers* will be Answered

INSIDE TRACK	MIDDLE LANES	FAST TRACK	
Monday: ☐ Isaiah 59:1-2; ☐ James 5:19	**Monday:** ☐ Romans 8:12-27 ☐ Proverbs 15:28-29 ☐ James 5: 13-18	**Monday:** ☐ Habakkuk 1:1-5 ☐ I Samuel 12:14-25 ☐ II Samuel 7:18-29 ☐ Mark 11:20-25 ☐ Acts 8:14-24 ☐ ☐	**RIGHTEOUS? OR SINNER?** _____ _____ _____ _____ _____
Tuesday: ☐ 1 John 5:14-17 ☐	**Tuesday:** ☐ Acts 12:1-16 ☐ Psalms 34:4-18 ☐ I John 3:19-22	**Tuesday:** ☐ I Samuel 1:1-20 ☐ Jonah 1:11-2:10 ☐ Luke 11:1-13 ☐ John 17:1-26 ☐ I Timothy 2:1-8 ☐ ☐	**GOD HEARS US** _____ _____ _____ _____ _____
Wednesday: ☐ James 4:1-4 ☐	**Wednesday:** ☐ Isaiah 1:1-15 ☐ Luke 18:1-14 ☐ I Corinthians 12:7-10	**Wednesday:** ☐ Deuteronomy 3:18-29 ☐ Psalms 22:1-20 ☐ I Samuel 28:3-19 ☐ II Samuel 12:1-25 ☐ Matthew 6:5-24 ☐ Luke 22:39-46 ☐	**UNANSWERED PRAYERS** _____ _____ _____ _____ _____
Thursday: ☐ Heb 4:14-16 ☐	**Thursday:** ☐ Psalms 86:1-17 ☐ Philippians 4:4-9 ☐ Acts 28:8-10	**Thursday:** ☐ Psalms 51:1-12 ☐ Psalms 54:1-7 ☐ Psalms 55:1-23 ☐ II Corinthians 1:8-11 ☐ Ephesians 6:10-20 ☐ ☐	**IN TIME OF NEED** _____ _____ _____ _____ _____
Friday: ☐ James 1:5-8 ☐	**Friday:** ☐ Luke 6:12-16 ☐ Ephesians 3:14-21 ☐ Acts 4:23-31	**Friday:** ☐ I Kings 3:3-14 ☐ Acts 10:1-33 ☐ I Corinthians 14:13-20 ☐ Ephesians 1:15-23 ☐ Philippians 1:3-11 ☐ Colossians 4:2-6 ☐	**ASK FOR WISDOM** _____ _____ _____ _____ _____

"A studious perusal of the sacred volume will make better citizens, better fathers, and better husbands"

-Thomas Jefferson

3rd Bible Reading Marathon

WEEK 22: [Dates:...........................] **PROMISES OF GOD:** *Salvation from Sin*

INSIDE TRACK	MIDDLE LANES	FAST TRACK	
Monday: ☐ Matt 7:21-23 ☐	**Monday:** ☐ 2 Corinthians 5:15-19 ☐ Matthew 28:18-20 ☐ Acts 10: 1-20	**Monday:** ☐ Ephesians 1:3-23 ☐ Acts 10: 34-48 ☐ Acts 22: 1-21 ☐ ☐ ☐ ☐	**AVAILABLE TO EVERYONE**
Tuesday: ☐ Rom 1:16-17 ☐	**Tuesday:** ☐ Romans 2:17-24 ☐ Romans 5: 6-17 ☐	**Tuesday:** ☐ Acts 4: 8-36 ☐ Colossians 3: 13-16 ☐ Romans 5:1-5 ☐ 1 Peter 4:1-6 ☐ ☐ ☐	**ACCESSED BY THE GOSPEL**
Wednesday: ☐ Acts 4:12 ☐	**Wednesday:** ☐ 1 Peter 3:20-22 ☐ Ephesians 2:8-9 ☐ Romans 12:1-10	**Wednesday:** ☐ Acts 2: 1-47 ☐ Acts 3:11-26 ☐ Acts 14:1-7 ☐ Acts 14:21-23 ☐ ☐ ☐	**JESUS SAVES**
Thursday: ☐ Matt 28:18-20	**Thursday:** ☐ Hebrews 5:7-10 ☐ Romans 1:14-17 ☐ Isaiah 12:1-3	**Thursday:** ☐ Acts 26:1-28 ☐ Galatians 3:26-29 ☐ Colossians 1:21-27 ☐ ☐ ☐ ☐	**BELIEVE & OBEY CHRIST**
Friday: ☐ Rev 2:9-11	**Friday:** ☐ Matthew 25:21-24 ☐ Phillipians 2:6-9 ☐ Acts 20-24	**Friday:** ☐ Luke 12: 40-42 ☐ 1 Peter 4:7-13 ☐ ☐ ☐ ☐ ☐	**BE FAITHFUL UNTIL DEATH**

"Hold fast to the Bible as the anchor of your liberties, write its precepts on your hearts and practice them in your lives"
-Ulysses S. Grant

3rd Bible Reading Marathon

WEEK 23: [Dates:...........................] **PROMISES OF GOD:** We have a *Hope*

INSIDE TRACK	MIDDLE LANES	FAST TRACK	
Monday:	**Monday:**	**Monday:**	**HOPE IS WAITING ON GOD**
☐ Rom 8:23-25	☐ Numbers 14:24-25	☐ James 5:7-11	
☐	☐ Joshua 14:6-15	☐ Psalms 37:7	
	☐	☐ Lamentations 3:25-26	
		☐ Psalms 40:1-3	
Tuesday:	**Tuesday:**	**Tuesday:**	**GOD CAN NOT LIE**
☐ Hebr 6:17-19	☐ Genesis 17:1-8	☐ Genesis 21:1-3	
☐	☐ Genesis 17:15-17	☐ Hebrews 11:11-12	
	☐ Genesis 18: 10-15	☐ Luke 1:54-55	
		☐ Romans 4:18-25	
		☐ Galatians 3:15-18	
Wednesday:	**Wednesday:**	**Wednesday:**	**AN ANCHOR OF THE SOUL**
☐ Romans 5:1-5	☐ Acts 27:23-44	☐ Psalms 119:27-28	
☐	☐	☐ 1 Thessalonians 5:5-11	
	☐	☐ Luke 6: 46-49	
		☐ Ephesians 3:14-21	
Thursday:	**Thursday:**	**Thursday:**	**ABOUND IN HOPE**
☐ Romans 15:13	☐ 1 Samuel 1:1-20	☐ 1 Samuel 2:1-10	
☐	☐	☐ Romans 15:13	
	☐	☐ Mark 7:24-30	
		☐ Psalms 25:3	
Friday:	**Friday:**	**Friday:**	**WORK UNTIL THE END**
☐ Hebr 6:11-12	☐ Luke 2:25-32	☐ 2 Peter 3:1-18	
☐	☐ Luke 2:36-38	☐ 2 Peter 1:10-15	
	☐	☐ Psalms 27:14	
		☐ Philippians 3:12-16	

"Men do not reject the Bible because it contradicts itself but because it contradicts them."

-E. Paul Hovey

3rd Bible Reading Marathon

WEEK 24: [Dates:..........................]   **PROMISES OF GOD:** *He Will not Forsake us*

INSIDE TRACK	MIDDLE LANES	FAST TRACK	
Monday:	**Monday:**	**Monday:**	**THE PROMISE**
☐ Hebrews 13:5-6	☐ I Kings 19: 9-14	☐ I Kings 19:15-18	
	☐ Daniel 6: 1-17	☐ Daniel 6: 18-26	
Tuesday:	**Tuesday:**	**Tuesday:**	**WHEN FEARFUL**
☐ Isaiah 41:10	☐ Joshua 7:1-12	☐ Joshua 7: 13-26	
	☐ Psalms 51	☐ Psalms 86	
Wednesday:	**Wednesday:**	**Wednesday:**	**WORRY AND ANXIETIES**
☐ Phil 4:6-7	☐ Matthew 6: 19-34	☐ John 6:28-40	
	☐ II Timothy 3:1-9	☐ Acts 27: 21-26	
		☐ II Timothy 3: 10-17	
Thursday:	**Thursday:**	**Thursday:**	**PERSONAL LOSS**
☐ John 14:1-2	☐ John 11:17-46	☐ II Samuel 1:1-27	
	☐ John 10: 17-44	☐ Job 1: 13-22	
Friday:	**Friday:**	**Friday:**	**FACING DEATH**
☐ Acts 27:22-24	☐ I John 1:1-4	☐ I John 5:1-21	
	☐ Deuteronomy 34: 1-12	☐ Revelation 21:22	
		☐ Revelation 22:5	
		☐ II Timothy 4:1-8	

"I have known ninety-five of the world's greatest men in my time, and of these eighty-seven were followers of the Bible.
-W.E. Gladstone

3rd Bible Reading Marathon

WEEK 25: [Dates:..........................] **PROMISES OF GOD:** *A Guaranteed Inheritance*

INSIDE TRACK	MIDDLE LANES	FAST TRACK	
Monday: ☐ Titus 1:1-2 ☐	**Monday:** ☐ Galatians 3:15-21 ☐ 2Peter 1:3-10 ☐	**Monday:** ☐ Hebrews 9:11-15 ☐ Romans 4:1-18 ☐ James 2:5 ☐ Hebrews 6:13-19 ☐ ☐ ☐	**THE PROMISE**
Tuesday: ☐ Eph 1:11-14 ☐	**Tuesday:** ☐ Romans 8:1-17 ☐ ☐	**Tuesday:** ☐ Galatians 4:1-7 ☐ 1 Peter 1:3-4 ☐ Ephesians 1:11-14 ☐ Revelation 21:1-7 ☐ John 17:20-26 ☐ ☐	**FOR THOSE IN CHRIST**
Wednesday: ☐ Acts 20:32 ☐	**Wednesday:** ☐ Matthew 25:31-46 ☐ ☐	**Wednesday:** ☐ 1 Corinthians 6:9-11 ☐ Romans 2:6-10 ☐ Acts 26:15-18 ☐ ☐ ☐ ☐	**THE SANCTIFIED**
Thursday: ☐ Titus 2:11-14 ☐	**Thursday:** ☐ Matthew 20:1-16 ☐ ☐	**Thursday:** ☐ Colossians 3:23-24 ☐ Galatians 3:6-9 ☐ 1 Timothy 6:17-19 ☐ 1 Corinthians 3:8-15 ☐ Colossians 1:9-14 ☐ ☐	**GOOD WORKS**
Friday: ☐ Revelation 2:10 ☐	**Friday:** ☐ Matthew 13:24-30 ☐ Matthew 13:36-43 ☐	**Friday:** ☐ Titus 3:3-7 ☐ 2 Timothy 4:6-8 ☐ James 1:9-12 ☐ 1 Corinthians 9:24-26 ☐ Revelation 3:11 ☐ ☐	**A CROWN OF LIFE**

"The Scriptures teach us the best way of living, the noblest way of suffering, and the most comfortable way of dying"

-John Flavel

Now, Do Something about it!

Tomorrow begins the last week of your Bible Reading Marathon *"run"*. You have stayed with it regardless of the time and effort required. For twenty-five weeks you have read some portion of God's Word that focused on "His Promises". If you took the *"fast track"* you will have actually read more than 6000 verses of Scripture. That's a notable act of faith and a statement about your sincerity in wanting to know the Will of God. Our congratulations!

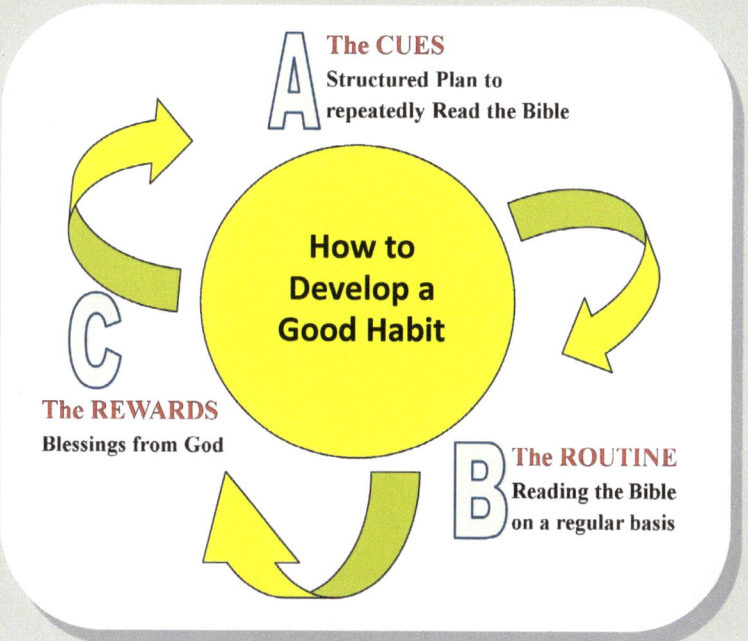

But actually the 26-week endurance "run" has only been a training to develop "the habit" of regular Bible reading! Do you remember the diagram above? It illustrates the ideas behind the Bible Reading Marathon. The Marathon is only a tool to get the job done!

After next week you will be on your own to set your own schedule at your own pace in practicing the habit of regular Bible reading. There are dozens of good plans available. Some plans will take you through the entire Bible in a year. Others are focused on specific topics or lines of thought. Or, you can use your regular Bible classes at church to form the outline for your reading. The important thing: READ GOD'S WORD REGULARLY!

But there is more…you must act on what you read! It is easy to "forget", remember only those who read God's Word and "DO IT" will be blessed! The *"doer"* will be blessed! That means just one thing: There is something you can do to be pleasing to God! Pure religion is more than just a stated set of beliefs, it is regularly practicing the things of God! Do it! Act on it! Make your behaviors change because of it! That's the final result from reading God's Word.

> "But he who looks into the perfect law of liberty and continues in it,
> and is not a forgetful hearer
> but a doer of the work,
> this one will be blessed in what he does."
> (James 1:25)

Bible Reading Marathon

WEEK 26: [Dates:............................] **PROMISES OF GOD:** *Eternal Life*

INSIDE TRACK	MIDDLE LANES	FAST TRACK	
Monday: ☐ John 14:1-3 ☐	**Monday:** ☐ Isaiah 51: 6-8 ☐ Isaiah 65: 17-25 ☐ John 14: 9-14	**Monday:** ☐ Romans 10: 4-17 ☐ Hebrews 6: 16-20 ☐ II Peter 3 ☐ ☐ ☐ ☐	**PREPARED BY JESUS**
Tuesday: ☐ John 5:28-29 ☐	**Tuesday:** ☐ Daniel 12: 1-3 ☐ Luke 12: 1-21 ☐	**Tuesday:** ☐ Luke 16: 19-31 ☐ Romans 2: 5-11 ☐ I Peter 1: 3-9 ☐ Revelation 20: 11-15 ☐ Revelation 21: 22-27 ☐ ☐	**IN HEAVEN OR HELL**
Wednesday: ☐ John 3:3-5 ☐	**Wednesday:** ☐ John 1: 1-18 ☐ Galatians 3: 26-29 ☐	**Wednesday:** ☐ Acts 22: 1-21 ☐ Titus 3: 3-7 ☐ I Peter 1: 13-25 ☐ I John 5: 1-11 ☐ ☐ ☐	**MUST BE BORN AGAIN**
Thursday: ☐ John 17:1-5 ☐	**Thursday:** ☐ Jeremiah 9: 23, 24 ☐ Psalms 100 ☐ John 12: 23-26	**Thursday:** ☐ John 14: 6, 7 ☐ Romans 1: 18-32 ☐ Romans 11: 33-36 ☐ Philippians 3: 12-21 ☐ I Thessalonians 1: 8-10 ☐ I John 4: 1-10 ☐	**TO KNOW GOD/CHRIST**
Friday: ☐ 1 Cor 15:51-54 ☐	**Friday:** ☐ Isaiah 25 ☐ Hosea 13:14 ☐	**Friday:** ☐ John 5: 24-27 ☐ Romans 8: 37-39 ☐ I Corinthians 15: 42-56 ☐ II Cointhians. 5: 10 ☐ Hebrews 2: 14,15 ☐ ☐	**VICTORY OVER DEATH**

"This Book will keep you from sin and only sin will keep you from this Book."

-D.L. Moody

Test your Skills at Translating the Bible?
Place an "X" before the one answer you consider to be the closest to the meaning of these English words

1. <u>Charity</u> never faileth (1 Corinthians 13:8)
   - ( ) help for the poor
   - ( ) affection
   - ( ) grace
   - ( ) love
2. Charity <u>suffereth long</u> (I Corinthians 13:4)
   - ( ) has pain for a long time
   - ( ) is patient
   - ( ) is content
   - ( ) never stops giving to the needy
3. Can the <u>children of the bridechamber</u> fast, while the bridegroom is with them? (Mark 2:19
   - ( ) friends of the bridegroom
   - ( ) young servants for the bride and groom
   - ( ) children from premarital relationships
   - ( ) children conceived in the bridechamber
4. And <u>straightway</u> he entered into a ship with his disciples (Mark 8:10)
   - ( ) walking straight
   - ( ) leaving a straight path
   - ( ) immediately
   - ( ) walking erectly
5. And <u>it came to pass in those days</u> that Jesus came from Nazareth of Galilee (Mark 1:9)
   - ( ) it moved through a narrow passage between the hills
   - ( ) Jesus walked through a pass among the hills
   - ( ) it happened quickly
   - ( ) at that time this occurred
6. Therefore if <u>any man</u> be in Christ, he is a new creature (2 Corinthians 5:17)
   - ( ) any adult male
   - ( ) any male
   - ( ) anyone
   - ( ) any creation
7. Only he who now <u>letteth</u> will let, until he be taken out of the way (2 Thessalonians 2:7)
   - ( ) permits
   - ( ) lets it happen
   - ( ) equalizes
   - ( ) restrains
8. For the word of God is <u>quick</u> and powerful, and sharper than any twoedged sword (Hebrews 4:12)
   - ( ) penetrating
   - ( ) living
   - ( ) fast-acting
   - ( ) convicting
9. The <u>dumb</u> ass speaking with man's voice forbad the madness of the prophet (2 Peter 2:16).
   - ( ) foolish
   - ( ) unintelligent
   - ( ) unable to speak
   - ( ) stupid
10. And he is the <u>propitiation</u> for our sins (1 John 2:2)
    - ( ) forgiveness
    - ( ) sacrifice
    - ( ) persuasion
    - ( ) judge
11. For this cause many are weak and sickly among you, and many <u>sleep</u> (1 Corinthians 11:30)
    - ( ) spiritual slumber
    - ( ) are lethargic
    - ( ) have died
    - ( ) are carnal
12. It is hard for thee to kick against the <u>pricks</u> (Acts 9:5)
    - ( ) very unpleasant persons
    - ( ) remorse
    - ( ) goads
    - ( ) splinters
13. And went to him, and <u>bound up his wounds, pouring oil and wine</u> (Luke 10:34
    - ( ) first bandaged his wounds, then poured oil and wine
    - ( ) first poured oil and wine, then bandaged
    - ( ) first bandaged, then gave him oil/wine as medicine
    - ( ) first bandaged, then offered a sacrifice to God
14. who for the joy set before him endured the cross <u>despising the shame</u> (Hebrews 12:2)
    - ( ) hated the shame
    - ( ) accepted the shame
    - ( ) hated shameful sins
    - ( ) loved shameful sinners
15. Then said Mary unto the angel, How shall this be, seeing I <u>know not a man</u> (Luke 1:34)
    - ( ) haven't met a man yet
    - ( ) don't know any men
    - ( ) am a virgin
    - ( ) am not acquainted with a man who can help
16. For the Kingdom of God is not <u>meat</u> and drink
    - ( ) meat
    - ( ) a good appetite
    - ( ) poultry
    - ( ) eating
17. The love of Christ <u>constraineth</u> us (2 Corinthians 5:14)
    - ( ) restrains
    - ( ) strains
    - ( ) encourages
    - ( ) compels
18. <u>Suffer</u> little children to come unto me (Mark 10:14)
    - ( ) put up with
    - ( ) suffer while
    - ( ) be patient while
    - ( ) allow
19. <u>Bring forth fruits meet for repentance</u> (Matthew 3:8)
    - ( ) cultivate fruit that will help people repent
    - ( ) repent so that you can bear fruit in your life
    - ( ) show by your actions that you have repented
    - ( ) bring forth fruits so that you can meet repentance
20. <u>rightly dividing</u> the word of truth (2 Timothy 2:15)
    - ( ) finding the right divisions
    - ( ) separating falsity from error
    - ( ) properly separating from those who falsely teach
    - ( ) accurately handling
21. It is good for a man not to <u>touch a woman</u> (1 Corinthians 7:1)
    - ( ) physically contact a woman
    - ( ) emotionally affect a woman
    - ( ) hug a woman
    - ( ) have sexual relations with a woman
22. <u>bewitched</u> the people of Samaria (Acts 8:9)
    - ( ) casts a spell on
    - ( ) amazed
    - ( ) bewildered
    - ( ) performed witchcraft on
23. The Lord is my Shepherd, <u>I shall not want</u>
    - ( ) not want anything else
    - ( ) not want anything I shouldn't
    - ( ) not lack anything
    - ( ) shall be content with whatever I have

Notes from your Readings

Notes from your Readings

Notes from your Readings

www.ingramcontent.com/pod-product-compliance
Lightning Source LLC
Chambersburg PA
CBHW041225040426

42444CB00002B/46